RESTAURANTEUR – PROTECT YOUR PROFITS!

DISCOVER RESTAURANT SCAMS AND
TECHNOLOGY SOLUTIONS

DON POTTER

Don Potter/Restauranteur – Protect Your Profits!
Printed in the United States of America

Restauranteur – Protect Your Profits!/ Don Potter -- 1st ed.

ISBN 978-0-692-04535-0 Print Edition

ISBN 978-0-692-04536-7 Ebook Edition

CONTENTS

INTRODUCTION

This book is intended for first-time restaurant proprietors—owners frustrated by a lack of profitability concerning their restaurants and restaurant investors.

I have run my own business for over twenty-five years and have also struggled with the profitability of my business. The business equation seems simple enough: sales or gross revenue minus costs and expenses equals your profit. However, there are many things that needlessly eat away at your profit. It's easy to compute your fixed costs like rent and utilities; however, other costs may be difficult to get a handle on.

In the early days of our business, we didn't have any controls in place to keep track of our inventory. Small computer parts, like disk drives and motherboards, weren't tracked. It wasn't until at least five years into the business that we realized our employees were using our equipment for their personal gain. It took us a while to establish inventory controls, but once we did, it helped us protect our income and improved our bottom-line results. Once we started tracking inventory employee, theft was almost negligible and our profitability increased.

We also tackled labor and management. When it's not monitored, overtime is a labor cost that can catch you by surprise. Overtime is something that's rarely anticipated, and it can kill your profit. I could go on for pages about similar things that reduced profitability my business, but we're here to talk about your business—a restaurant.

I've never run or owned a restaurant, but I have worked with restauranteurs for over twenty-five years. My company provides business solutions that enable owners to improve their operations and—more importantly—improve their profitability. My company sells and implements restaurant point of sale (POS) systems, software tools for inventory and labor management, loss prevention products, and much more.

Over those twenty-five years, I have worked closely with restaurant owners who have consulted with me and explained their problems; I've learned a lot from these restaurateurs. They've told me of their problems, from their operational snags to dealing with employee theft and a whole host of scams. I have gained considerable knowledge on how technology and management systems, when properly implemented, can help eliminate the restaurant's profit-killers and improve the bottom-line profits. In speaking directly with restaurant managers and owners, we have developed solutions to address their specific needs.

Restaurateurs have outlined their business problems and their preferred solutions to those challenges. Ultimately, they all wanted to boost their restaurants' profitability. I remember restaurant owners recounting stories from the frontline, explaining why they needed a certain software feature. I watched as those features and tools were developed and implemented with great success. Not everyone knows these tools are available or understands how to implement them.

This book details critical aspects of running a restaurant from best practices to managing loss prevention. We'll look at each area of your restaurant business to identify where you can benefit from implementing best practices along with tried and tested technology tools. You may encounter topics that seem obvious, while also discovering things that never crossed your mind.

My hope is you will gain some valuable takeaways that will improve the profitability of your restaurant. You'll also have a handy reference guide to use whenever you consider upgrading or improving your in-house technology. Finally, I hope you have some fun reading the stories I've collected over the years.

Best Practices and Scams

How can you minimize errors and omissions while eliminating theft and scams?

I entered the world of restaurant POS by circumstance. I had transferred to Florida with a large computer company, but after a year the company closed my branch office and planned to send me up north to their Tampa branch. Knowing I wanted to stay in South Florida, I searched for a way to earn a living there. Through a friend, I heard about a computer-based POS system that had been developed in my home state of Rhode Island. The company, Restaurant Data Concepts, was looking for resellers to sell and support their product, known as POSitouch[1]. I was interested in learning more, so I reached out to them.

Restaurant Data Concepts was founded in Pawtucket, Rhode Island. By the time I was introduced to POSitouch in 1989, it had already been fully functional and successfully working in many restaurants for several years. I liked that it was an open system and not dependent on proprietary hardware or tied to a specific computer or peripheral device. I was also impressed the company's three founders had backgrounds that complemented each other: one was a software developer, one was a successful restauranteur, and the third was a certified public accountant (CPA).

---

1 POSitouch was acquired by the Lighthouse Network in October 2017.

They made a good team. The software developer created the restaurant POS software that was both functional and flexible. The restaurateur ensured the software worked properly and wouldn't impede service. The CPA insisted on complete accountability by implementing strict audit trails.

The first time I saw POSitouch in operation, I was truly amazed. It was at a seasonal restaurant in Rhode Island called Ballard's—located on the water where the Block Island ferry docks. Ballard's was a large restaurant with an extensive menu and busy bar. As I witnessed the POSitouch system in action, I watched a ten-terminal system working at full speed with every terminal in use—checks printing, cash drawers popping—all running on a little 286-based personal computer. There were servers entering orders and bartenders serving patrons. It was much simpler and faster than other typical keyboard systems I had seen to date. I was amazed at how smoothly everything was working.

I didn't know much about restaurants at that point, but I was impressed with the system from a technology standpoint. I had sold accounting and distribution computer systems to general businesses, so I knew what a business computer solution could do to improve profitability. I was sure this was a leading product I could get going back in Florida. I was so impressed with POSitouch that I became the third value-added reseller (VAR) for POSitouch in September of 1989. A VAR or POS dealer represents the software developer and provides restaurant-operating clients with all the software and hardware—along with training installation and ongoing support. This was my entry into the restaurant industry.

In December of 1989, we sold our first system to a fast-paced operation with a full bar and kitchen. The restaurant was located on the Intracoastal Waterway in Fort Lauderdale. It had a full menu and two busy bars. On weekends, it jammed with live entertainment.

Two partners owned the operation and were onsite part time. Thinking back, I don't know whether it was my outstanding salesmanship or the partners' keen ability to assess the benefits of the POS system that prompted them to buy one. Either way, the owners realized they could gain greater control of their operation and protect their profits by purchasing the POS system.

The system was installed in their busy waterfront restaurant in December at the beginning of the tourist season. This was the first time I had installed a system in a restaurant, so there was a learning curve for my team, as well as the restaurant staff that was used to hand-writing orders. The servers would write the food and drinks on a ticket to record the items and menu price. They would then take the ticket to the kitchen and place it on a board or a rack, so the kitchen staff would know what to make.

The new system was completely different. The wait staff had to adjust to entering their orders into the computer. The computer would automatically print the orders in the kitchen. The managers' duties changed as well, including approving all voids and comps. The old way was to verbally approve the void or comp; now they had to record each instance into the computer with their credentials and who they were performing the transaction for.

The first month was touch and go. The employees blamed the POS system for every problem that arose. If a server made a mistake, or if the kitchen was slow, it was the POS's fault. Some staff members resisted the new POS system and complained to the owners the system slowed them down, resulting in poor customer service. They also claimed they were having problems with it. The owners asked me to come in several times to observe and troubleshoot the system on busy nights. Of course, everything went smoothly when I was there.

Just when I thought things were settling down at the waterfront restaurant, I received a call from one of the owners. He explained to me that the POS system was working very well for food orders, but it was a disaster in the bar. I asked him why he thought it was only problematic at the bar. He told me that Eddy, the general manager, had complained. He claimed that because the bartenders now had to enter every drink into the POS system, it delayed service. Sometimes guests were so upset with the slow service, they would storm out with unpaid tabs. He added that guests poked fun at the new system and claimed it ruined the atmosphere.

"Overall, the POS system is bad for business," said the owner. I assured him I would do whatever he wanted. I also told him it didn't make sense to have a POS system that would only work for the food operation but not for the bar. It wasn't a good conversation. I felt terrible. I could just imagine how competitors would react to the news the restaurant was removing the POS system from the bar. I knew I could show him how fast the system worked, and he'd keep it installed. He agreed to meet with me to discuss his concerns, and I could show him how it worked. Then we would be able to reach a mutually beneficial solution.

I met with the owner not knowing what to expect. He reiterated that Eddy said they were losing business because the POS system slowed down the bartenders so much the guests would leave in frustration. To ensure I understood the issue, I restated Eddy's complaint. "He says it takes too long to enter in the drinks. Is that correct?" He agreed.

Since it was morning and the restaurant was closed, I suggested we head over to the bar and practice using the system. I would act as the bartender and attempt to duplicate the problem. I approached the POS terminal and asked the owner to give me a typical drink order. He ordered some pretend drinks and cocktails from me, and

I touched the drink order on the POS screen. He could instantly see the process was easy and fast. It was certainly faster than writing down many drinks on a long tab. I demonstrated the POS system didn't hinder the bartender at all. With a concerned expression, he asked me why I thought Eddy would claim the POS system was so slow. I told him I didn't know why he'd perceive the system that way. In that moment, I think he figured out why Eddy was unhappy with the system.

> **The POS didn't just exist to make things faster and easier; its greatest purpose was to protect the owner's profits.**

Immediately following my demonstration, Eddy arrived. He greeted me with a scowl. The owner made small talk and invited Eddy to go out with him and some friends on Wednesday night. Eddy said he couldn't make it because he was scheduled to bartend. The owner said, "You're the general manager. Why are you bartending?" I don't remember Eddy's response, but I do recall that I finally understood why Eddy was complaining about the system. Eddy disliked the fact the POS system gave the owner so much control over the inventory. This impinged on Eddy's ability to run scams.

There was a complete audit trail of everything that was ordered and processed. Any changes or deletions would be recorded for the owner's review. This exchange between Eddy and the owner was enlightening for me. I had an aha moment and understood the true purpose of the POS system. This was a cash business with a great deal of exposure to theft and fraud. The POS didn't just exist to make things faster and easier; its greatest purpose was to protect the owner's profits. Incidentally, Eddy was fired two weeks later. The restaurant has since changed hands, and the POS system is still in place protecting their profits.

The POS system has many features and benefits. In the restaurant business, like so many other businesses, there's resistance to new ways of doing things, even when the benefits are evident. I'm surprised by the number of bars that still use old cash registers. I wonder what keeps owners tied to the technology of cash registers. Cash registers were perfected by the National Cash Register company (NCR) back in the late 1800s. If owners are going to insist on cash registers, why don't they just ditch their cars and ride a horse to work?

In all seriousness, I've heard some owners like to operate on a cash basis. Some even know the bartenders dip their hands in the till and are silent partners. Many accept it, as long as the bartenders don't take too much. A surprising number of owners have been convinced by their bartenders a POS system will slow them down, and they'll lose business.

Owners' primary concerns when running a bar are loss of revenue and product theft. In fact, the two go hand in hand. It's critical to prevent bartenders from pocketing your money and giving away your product or inventory. These are the most common frauds carried out by bartenders that reduce your revenue and increase theirs.

This is how it works. A customer orders two beers and the bartender says, "That will be six dollars." The customer hands him eight dollars and grabs the beers. The bartender turns to the POS or the cash register, hits the "no sale" button, puts the dollar in the drawer, places seven dollars in the tip jar, and rings the tip bell. In short, the bartender doesn't ring up the transaction and keeps the cash. Your product is given away, and the profit goes to the bartender. The no-sale button has been a feature available on cash registers to give bartenders the ability to make change for clients, so they could use vending machines or leave tips.

Some POS systems have a pole display that faces the customers and displays the transactions while the bartender rings up the order.

This is to let the bartender know someone is watching what they're doing. Even in the scenario above, the bartender may ring up the two beers so the system displays the transaction, but then he may "delete" the transaction before it is completed. The ability to delete an item is usually available on the POS system, because if the bartender makes a mistake, they'll need to remove or delete it.

Let's say the customer orders two Budweisers, and the bartender accidentally touches two Bud Lights; then the two Bud Lights must be removed or deleted. If your system records what was deleted at the POS, then you'll be able to see how many deletes are occurring. If bartenders usually have an average of six deletes per shift, but the new bartender has twenty-six, there may be a problem. The bottom line is your products are not being sold, but rather they've been given away. That will kill your profit.

One of the ways to counter this is to control your inventory during each shift. For example, if the bartender starts with 100 beers at the beginning of the shift and ends with twenty, then eighty beers must be accounted for. This can get complicated when there are many bars and bartenders.

Another approach is to set up your POS system to record each of the bartender's no-sale transactions. Then search all requests. If you note at the end of the shift an average bartender has two or three no sales per shift, and you see the new bartender is averaging twenty per shift with lower than average sales, you may have a problem.

Even with strict inventory control at the bar, problems can still exist. One such example is the short pour. When drinking a cocktail at a restaurant or bar, how many times have you wondered: *Where's the alcohol?* You may have been the victim of a short pour. Clever bartenders can scam the bar with a short pour.

Here's how the short pour works. Let's take the most popular alcohol: vodka. The house pour for vodka is 1.5 ounces. Every time a bartender pours a mixed drink with vodka, he short pours by .5 ounces. After three pours, the bartender has saved enough vodka to give away a "free" drink or sell a drink and pocket the money. He says to a lucky customer, "This one's on me," to increase his tip or to sell it on a cash transaction and take the money. When the inventory is checked, everything will be accounted for, but your establishment may get a bad rap for overpriced drinks.

The more complex systems offer sophisticated controls and processes that increase control and bottom-line profitability for your restaurant.

I heard from a client about another scam where a bartender smuggled in his own bottle of vodka in a duffle bag and sold his own drinks all night. When the inventory was checked, it was all accounted for. Another employee revealed the scam to the owner. And even though the owner ended the scam by firing the bartender, the owner didn't know how long he had been getting away with it.

The Basic POS System

There are many different POS systems on the market. They range from very simple cash registers, keyboard systems, and tablets to comprehensive touchscreen computers systems. The basic computer systems can perform the simple operation of printing a price on a check. The more complex systems offer sophisticated controls and processes that increase control and bottom-line profitability for your restaurant.

Here are some things to consider when looking at a POS system for your business. When looking at POS functionality, how can you minimize the two primary profit killers? How can you minimize errors and omissions, while eliminating theft and scams?

Pricing Control

You will program your POS system with the correct pricing for the items you plan to sell. If you sell an item at the same price throughout the day, all systems will work for you. If your operation includes special pricing based on the time of day or day of the week, you will need to more carefully evaluate the system you're purchasing.

For example, if you have happy hour pricing for your bar drinks, the system you're purchasing should include price control based on your happy hour pricing schedule. Let's say your happy hour goes from 5:00 p.m. to 7:00 pm. Relying on your staff to sell the drinks at the regular price when happy hour ends is a potential problem that could impact your profitability. For example, you don't want your bartender to tell a customer that even though happy hour has ended, *wink wink*, he will honor the happy hour price. This would fall under the category of a theft or a scam.

There will be instances when the price of products will vary depending on the day of the week. Or you may offer bar entertainment that you're charging for. Like in the previous example, you wouldn't want your staff to be responsible for the price change; rather, you'd set up the system to control the price change.

When it comes to pricing control, it's best to have a system that handles all your pricing options that vary by day and time of day. Once you've set it up correctly, the system will track and generate the correct pricing.

Let's say a customer has a tab open, and she has been ordering drinks at the happy hour price. When the happy hour time shift occurs in the computer system, it will automatically revert to the non-discounted price. In other words, no human intervention is required

> **This guarantees that will receive the proper price for your drinks, never having to rely on your staff to do the right thing.**

to ensure the customer's check reflects the correct pricing. This guarantees you will receive the proper price for your drinks, never having to rely on your staff to do the right thing.

Requisition Control

When an order is placed in the POS system, it generates a requisition slip, more commonly known as a prep slip, in the kitchen or wherever it is processed. This is a simple process; if you ring up an item, it prints in the kitchen. Nothing should leave the kitchen unless a slip has been printed for it. Most restaurants I've worked with perform this basic function for main items, like entrees and appetizers; however, they don't always make sure everything that's rung up produces a requisition slip. These are often missed items on prep slips.

Most POS systems will track each item ordered through the POS. Any items ordered cannot be deleted or taken out of the system without a manager's intervention. Managers must enter their distinct pass code into the POS and review the transaction before using a delete, comp, or discount function for an item. The POS records all the details of the transaction—the specific guest check, the specific server, and the specific manager who performed the function. The POS recording these functions gives the ownership all necessary audit trails to see what's going on in their restaurant.

While this may seem pretty basic, there are many restaurants that don't insist everything be printed on a requisition or prep slip. Examples include added-on items, such as extra cheese, sour cream, or guacamole. Many restaurant owners simply trust the servers and kitchen staff to include additional items on the check, but they can't always count on their employees to do the right thing. This problem is solved by setting up the POS system to require each item be added to the check and sent to the kitchen on a requisition slip.

In some restaurants, servers are responsible for getting certain items themselves, such as nonalcoholic beverages. Once again, owners rely on the servers to add the beverages to the customers' checks. But the reality is that even the best servers, on the best day, may fail to add a beverage to a customer's check, because they were too busy. The worst-case scenario is the server who approaches a table, smiles, and says, "Oh, don't worry. I took care of your beverage for you," looking to increase her tip. The server gives away something that wasn't hers to give away.

We performed an analysis for one restaurant where servers got their own beverages. We asked the owner for his assessment of how many beverages were omitted from customer checks on any given day. With eight servers on his staff, he figured at least two beverages per server per day were not making it onto the checks. His average drink price was two dollars. By doing the simple math, he calculated that 8 x 2 x $2 or $32 per day was not added to his bottom line. This is equivalent to $32 per day x 365 days equals $11,680 annually. He also calculated that items such as sour cream, extra cheese, and guacamole, which were not being tracked or requisitioned by the kitchen, accounted for another six to ten dollars per day in lost revenue.

Some POS systems can track beverages or items the servers get themselves, such as coffee, soda, or tea. This feature also prevents a guest check from being printed unless the number of beverages matches the guest count. If a guest does not want a beverage, the server must ring up either a "no beverage" or a "water" key. The POS reporting makes it easy to track the servers giving away beverages versus the ones who are ringing them up.

At the end of every shift, the POS can produce a cash-out report that shows you how many guests each server had compared to how many known beverages were sold. A typical cash out may show Mary had thirty guests with only two no-beverage guests during her shift, while John had thirty guests with sixteen no-beverage guests during his shift. Of course, there are customers who decide not to have a beverage with their meal—an average that can be determined from sales history. Once you determine the average number, you can compare that to all the other servers. You'll be able to see a trend of which server has the most no-beverage entries during each shift. You can now drill down into each server's numbers and determine why that server is either not selling beverages or not ringing them up—and compare that to everyone else.

Order Entry Control

The more selections and options your menu offers, the more control you'll need over the ordering process. For example, when a customer orders a sandwich plate there will likely be many associated options.

If you have a comprehensive menu with many modifiers and options, it's important to have a POS system that steps servers through the ordering process and ensures every question, modifier, and option are addressed for each given item.

He must select the bread—white or pumpernickel, plain or toasted—and toppings, including tomatoes, onions, and cheese, and then he must select a side, such as fries or coleslaw. Because building a sandwich plate can be complicated, you must ensure that the end product is exactly what the customer ordered. Any deviation from the order may result in an unsatisfied customer and a return of the item to the kitchen—which is wasted profit. Not only that, when you serve a mistake to your customer that's returned to the kitchen, it will most likely slow down the kitchen and effect the table turn, or the number of guests you can get through your restaurant. In addition, the server must re-take the order, and the kitchen must prepare a new meal. This slows down service. Instead the patron should've been finishing his meal, paying the bill, and leaving your restaurant as a satisfied customer.

If you have a comprehensive menu with many modifiers and options, it's important to have a POS system that steps servers through the ordering process and ensures every question, modifier, and option are addressed for each given item. A superior POS system will prevent the servers from deviating from this order-taking roadmap. In other words, the system makes it impossible for them to order the wrong thing, because multiple layers of options and modifiers can be set for each of your menu items.

I recommend that you program your most difficult menu items into the POS system to demonstrate how they'll display when rung up on the system. In addition, during the setup, all modifiers and options should be made accessible to servers, so they can't deviate or complete their orders without answering all necessary questions.

Other Considerations

It is also important the restaurant software is easy to learn and to use.

- Are the interfaces of the system intuitive?
- Can they be used without making too many errors?
- Can mistakes be easily corrected?
- Does it keep a proper audit trail?

New employees come and go constantly. The time it takes to become familiar and comfortable with the relevant functions of the system is a real cost. It's the overhead the restaurant owner must pay before an employee can become productive. You don't want a long and painful learning process, especially for new employees during their first Friday night dinner rush.

We are moving toward a cashless society. If the software provides cheap credit and debit processing, it can result in substantial savings to your operation. The POS system must also provide secure credit card processing, as customers are more sensitive these days to the risk of fraud and identity theft. Credit card processing is discussed in detail in Chapter 6.

The POS should have provisions for remote management. The restaurant owner or manager should be able to monitor and control the system off site. Finally, the vendor, either directly or through the VAR, should provide regular updates to the software, continually fixing any bugs and delivering improvements. There should be help with training and emergency support if the system fails.

Management Controls

It is best to choose a system that gives you transaction data on who- what- when- and where.

We received a call from a controller of a very busy restaurant who was earning just under five million dollars in revenue a year. He said, "We'd like you to go into the system and print six months of reports."

The request caught us by surprise, because this is something they could have done themselves. "I'm happy to do that, but you know you can do that yourself—right?" I said.

"No, we need you to do it. This is a legal case."

My heart raced. "Oh, are you suing us?"

"No, no, it's nothing like that. We believe an employee has been stealing from us."

"I'm sorry to hear that. The reports will help you determine if that's the case."

Comping Checks

One function in a POS system is voiding, deleting, or comping a transaction after it is rung up in the system. For example, if we serve a customer a steak, and it's too tough or wasn't cooked properly and the customer complains, a manager must remove that item from the patron's check and delete it. In the process of running a restaurant, mistakes happen, and to handle those mistakes to customers' satisfaction, owners allow managers to remove items from a check. It has, no doubt, happened to you. Your meal wasn't prepared well, and you said something like, "I can't eat this. It's burnt." In response, the server or the manager said, "Hey, no problem. We're going to take that off the check."

Most managers have the authority to comp checks. They not only comp checks when a meal is unsatisfactory, they may also choose to comp a check for a special customer, like a policeman or the mayor. Even though an item, like an entree, is rung up and accounted for, it must be deleted from the check. The restaurant used its inventory to prepare the meal for a customer, took the prepared food from the kitchen, and then a check was used to ring up the meal.

Most systems track voids and deletes with varying degrees of detail. Some systems simply show, for example, that the deletes totaled $100 on a given day; whereas a more sophisticated system would tell you the date, time, manager, and server who performed the deletion.

We told the controller who had contacted us we would produce a manager activity report showing six months of transactions. A manager activity report shows the manager who made the deletion, the server for whom he deleted it, the amount, and all the other details. As we presented the data to the controller, he determined over the five or six-month period, one of the restaurant's best managers was running a scam.

The manager had apparently convinced some servers, who he was friendly with, that the computer was having problems with settling cash checks. He told the servers to bring the check and customer's cash to him, and he would settle it for them. We're not certain whether or not the servers were in on the scam. The servers would take their tips out of the customer's cash and give the rest to the manager, who was supposedly settling the cash and putting the money in a cash drawer. Instead, he deleted the check by comping it, claimed the customer received a bad meal, and pocketed the cash. He ran the scam for months. In a restaurant like theirs that was hot, trendy, and rolling in the money, the loss didn't seem significant considering their profits.

The manager was skimming around $5,000 per month. With the volume of business, the numbers of voids and comps seemed normal and didn't set off any alarm bells.

The owners were making good money, so the scam went under the radar. In fact, it wasn't from a profit and loss statement or a sales report which tipped them off; every month it showed they were profitable. Rather than doing $420,000 in revenue that month, they did $415,000 in revenue. It wasn't a big number on the top line or the bottom line. This scam could've continued if a server, who wasn't part of the scam, hadn't caught wind of it. She approached the owners and said, "Hey, I just wanted to let you know, for some reason this manager makes servers give them their cash checks. I don't think that's right." She blew the whistle on the manager.

When it got back to management, they reviewed the activity report, which revealed all the comps were coming from the same manager and servers. We learned later, the young manager had an expensive cocaine addiction, so he figured out a way to scam the system.

Although this restaurant was operating at a profit, they weren't earning at their full potential. Even though the system could generate management activity reports, they weren't scrutinizing their reports. One recommended best practice is to not only look at sales and cash, but also the report when you're closing out the day. They weren't doing that.

Unfortunately, some people running restaurants don't want to install a system, because the manager is producing a monthly profit and the owner is happy. In some cases, the owner says, "I don't care if the manager is stealing a little bit, because I'm making enough." Those managers are the ones who typi- cally resist having a system put in, be- cause they don't want the increased accountability.

The bottom line: You must inspect the restaurant processes and transac- tions at every level. You must also make sure you have a system that shows you more than just your total, like a regular

> **The bottom line: you must inspect the res- taurant processes and transactions at every level.**

cash register would, which might show you that on a given day your comps and voids totaled $1,000.

It's best to choose a system that gives you transaction data on who, what, when, and where. For example, you would see—at a giv- en time—a manager and server performed a deletion associated with a specific check with a reason for the deletion. If it was because the steak served to a customer was bad, you must check with the kitchen and ask if they had any steaks returned on the shift in question.

Checks and balances exist. Unfortunately, many restaurants don't worry about it if they're profitable. In the case of the trendy restau- rant, the scam didn't come up as a red flag until someone blew the whistle. Their accountant didn't say, "Hey, boss, we're down 2% prof- it. What's going on?" That wasn't the red flag. The red flag came from a whistle blower.

It should be part of your daily routine to ask, "How much cash will we deposit in our bank account? How many credit card transac- tions do we have?" The daily routine should include reviewing your management alerts to see where you may have a potential theft or scam, as both are very common in the restaurant business.

One reason our industry is vulnerable to scams is that anyone can open a restaurant. For example, a guy cashes out his auto-shop business, because his long-held dream is to open his own restaurant and bar. He buys a restaurant, but the only industry he knows is the auto-shop business. The restaurant business is completely different; there's a lot more cash and moving parts than in most small businesses.

> Have a system that will not only report the voids, but will also show who performed them, the date and time, the server, and the check number.

The POS system we sell is installed in every Cheesecake Factory and Outback Steak House, and many other popular chains use it as well. It's very robust and loaded with features to prevent scams. There are many systems on the market; it's important to have a system that will not only report the voids, but will also show who performed them, the date and time, the server, and the check number.

With the introduction of the Cloud, there are new systems with built-in alerts that notify management when something happens. For example, an owner will receive an alert when a manager has voided or discounted a check. Using the Cloud, it's easier to monitor the POS system and manager transactions.

Coupons and Discounts

Another scam restaurant staff run involves coupons and discounts. Most restaurants offer discounts and coupons to drive customer demand, reward patrons, and increase business. For example, you might offer a discount to certain patrons, like policemen and firemen, or public officials. Or perhaps you run a discount available to all customers by offering coupons in the newspaper.

To be effective, there should always be an audit trail on a discount or coupon. Without an audit trail, a server can take advantage of coupons. It would work like this: The server clips the coupon and waits for a customer to pay with cash. The server doesn't tell the customer about the discount, so the customer pays the full amount of the check. The server applies the five-dollar coupon to the check and pockets the five dollars. The restaurant manager or owner thinks: *Wow! That coupon was really successful. Twenty people came in with the coupon. We've hit a home run!* But the truth is that an employee is using the coupon to steal cash from the restaurant.

> **To be effective, there should always be an audit trail on a discount or coupon.**

There are controls you can put in place to prevent such abuses. Before you apply the coupon, put a system in place that only allows managers to apply the coupons. Many restaurants now have loyalty systems that distribute coupons to customers only after they've registered. The loyalty programs are harder to scam. Restaurant owners are becoming savvier about employee scams, but there are still many who are naive; they open a small restaurant and find out the hard way.

Whenever you're tendering cash, you must watch out for scams related to comps, discounts, deletions, and coupons. A sophisticated system must have those controls, but unless you check it, go through the reports, and know what to look for on a consistent basis, there's the possibility for scamming.

The nature of some people is if there's an opportunity to scam and make an extra buck, they can't resist the temptation. The restaurant business has historically been a cash business and since the inventory is edible, the cash and the inventory often go missing—if they're not carefully monitored.

Sales Reporting

Sales reporting starts at a high level and drills down into detailed information. Any system reports how much you sold in a day and breaks down the sales into categories, such as food, beverages, and alcoholic beverages. Then, within those categories there are sub-categories. For example, the subcategories: Appetizers, salads, and entrees are included in the category of food. In the beverage category, the reporting would show how many iced teas, soft drinks, and waters were sold. And within the category of alcohol, the subcategories would show how much beer, liquor, and wine were sold. Finally, the subcategories can be further broken down into individual units.

> **A good system will generate any sales reports owners and managers want to see.**

A good system will generate any sales reports owners and managers want to see such as overall sales, as well as sales of food, alcoholic beverages, and nonalcoholic beverages. The reports answer the question:

"What products are selling?"

If you're not reviewing detailed sales reports, you're missing data on the items that are selling and the ones that aren't. If you're not analyzing your sales down to item details, you may be carrying items that aren't selling well and stocking the ingredients for them. In other words, you're missing opportunities to upgrade your menu by adding items that would sell and by removing items that aren't selling.

Then, when you drill down to the profit per item, if you're doing food costing, you can see which items are the most profitable. That's the difference between a cash register POS and a POS solution; you're implementing a business solution that enables you to determine your profitability on a per-item basis. You may have something on the menu that's an old favorite—the one that helped you launch the restaurant—but over time people have grown tired of it, and they're not buying it anymore. Nonetheless, it remains on your menu, because you don't have access to the right sales data.

The other aspect of a sales report is who is selling. In a restaurant, you may have twelve servers on the floor—each selling at different levels. One server approaches her customers by saying, "Hi! Can I take your order? Do you want any appetizers?" Alternatively, a different server approaches her customers by saying, "Hey, we have a great calamari dish people love. Would you like to try it?" The suggestive sales approach is more likely to entice customers to order the recommended dish.

If you analyze your sales by server, you can identify the server who produces the most revenue on any given shift. The sales report identifies the best salespeople over time. And then, based on their sales, you can cull the bottom ones. The top three servers are bringing in a high check average, and the bottom three servers are not. With the server sales report, you have the data you need to determine what the three bottom servers are doing wrong. The report indicates they have the same number of customers and tables, but they're not selling appetizers, desserts, or alcohol—items that can increase the check average.

With data in hand, you can assess the qualities or actions that contribute to your servers' success. Perhaps one server has a nice personality or offers enticing recommendations to customers. To improve sales among all servers, you may want to run contests in which you reward the servers for sales.

When inexperienced owners open a restaurant, their notion is that their restaurant will offer delicious food and fabulous drinks at reasonable prices, and they'll make good money. Some assume anybody can open a restaurant; it looks so simple. All you do is cook food and sell beer—right? Wrong. It's actually much harder than it seems. The TV show *Bar Rescue*, with food and beverage industry consultant Jon Taffer, features some of these owners who are naive about running a restaurant and struggling mightily. Within two or three days, he turns the whole operation around.

Many small restauranteurs don't know what tools are available to them to help them run a successful enterprise. Big chain restaurants, like Cheesecake Factory or Outback Steakhouse, already know how to effectively monitor and analyze sales. I could never tell a Cheesecake Factory or Outback Steakhouse manager something they don't already know. It's the small, independent restaurant owners who need this critical information. Some of them will figure it out on their own, but I want to shortcut that process. Instead of a reactive approach, such as, "Oh, we got screwed by our manager; we're never going let that happen again," I offer the prevention beforehand and give new restauranteurs pointers about the things they should be considering. Whether or not they choose to implement those considerations is up to them.

A typical restaurateur will spend more money on a tropical fish tank, a stereo system, or an LCD TV than installing the right POS system that will run his business and safeguard his profits. POS systems should be viewed like a normal operating expense. Take electricity, for example—something every restaurant requires. Let's say a restaurant's electricity bill is $500 a month in a restaurant with hoods and ovens. The electric company isn't going to say to the restaurant, "You're going to be in business for five years; that's $6,000 each year, multiplied over five years. Give me $30,000." The restaurant will pay monthly as it uses the electricity, which is the same thing as a POS system. A restaurant can get an operating lease and pay monthly.

Payment plans are available for any size restaurant and their unique budgetary requirements. Small restaurants don't have to buy the system outright, but the payment plan will cost less than paying a manager to run the restaurant. Unlike employees, the system will never call in sick or steal from you.

Audit Trails

An audit trail tracks voids, deletes, and comps. The audit trail tracks the specific employee who performed the void, delete, or comp, as well as the manager and the server associated with the check. There are scenarios in which managers collude with servers and make cash checks disappear. The audit trail would track transactions, ensuring checks and cash don't mysteriously disappear.

If you're evaluating systems for your restaurant, you should ensure audit trails is one of the features included, not just to show you overall deletes, but also who performed the delete, for which server it was performed, and the reason for the deletion. This is an important part of your audit trail you should inspect daily. Inspecting on a weekly basis is acceptable, but it's not ideal. You certainly wouldn't want to wait more than a week to go through your voids and deletes when looking for trends and patterns.

It's quite normal on occasion for a patron to receive a bad dinner. In this case, a server might say to you, "What was I supposed to do? I want them to come back, so I comped them the meal and took it off their check." You should have checks and balances in place to ensure that the comp actually occurred, as opposed to the server simply claiming the customer had a bad meal, then when the customer paid their check the server removed the meal from the check and pocketed the cash.

> **With the POS system, you'll have the confidence that your products and profits are protected.**

An audit trail inspects transactions and captures check details, so if a customer contacts you with a problem, you can pull up and review the check detail. For example, a customer calls and says, "I had dinner at your restaurant last night and got really sick afterwards. I think it was food poisoning." With an audit trail, you can call up the check detail to see exactly what the customer had and tie the check to a specific transaction. Then you can remedy the situation according to your restaurant policies.

The management controls in the POS system enable you to track, monitor, and analyze sales, including performance monitoring of your menus and sales staff. The system flags irregularities and helps you prevent thefts and scams common to the restaurant business. With the POS system, you'll have the confidence that your products and profits are protected.

Tax Preparation Support

Handling the challenges of tax preparation is a major aspect of running a food service business. Without a good restaurant management system, an establishment can easily be crushed beneath a mountain of tax-related paperwork. A good software system organizes the information your accountant will need to make tax return preparation much less painful.

Payroll taxes must be collected from all full and part-time employees to pay for Social Security and Medicare. Employees should report their tips which, in turn, must be reported by the restaurant owner. Sales taxes must be collected on all food and beverages. Some taxes are included in the price of items, while other taxes are added to the subtotal of each bill. Property and liquor license taxes must be paid. The better your system organizes your tax-related information, the easier your life will be at tax time.

Inventory Control: There is No Free Lunch

Poorly managed inventory and labor are the top two reasons restaurants go out of business.

Lack of tracking food cost is one of the major reasons restaurants go out of business. It occurs when you don't keep track of your inventory. As a result, you spend too much on your inventory and fail to get the return you need to stay in business. This chapter outlines why it is critical for restauranteurs to control their inventory to keep food cost in line, and presents the best practices for doing so.

Most restauranteurs know they must watch their food cost. Keeping track of food cost is an accounting function, where at the end of the month restaurant owners look at their invoices and ask themselves questions like: *What did I spend on liquor? How much did I spend on turkey breast? What did I spend on steak? How much did I spend on produce?* Invoices reflect the actual money spent on food and drinks. But what restauranteurs don't typically know is how much of their inventory they should have used, which is just as important as what they spent.

A problem inventory control uncovers in the restaurant industry is waste. Food waste occurs when food doesn't get portioned correctly, spoils, or falls on the floor. Your food invoice is not going to reflect waste; the invoice will simply show you what you spent.

Let's use turkey breast as an example to illustrate the need to go beyond simply using invoices for inventory control. Your invoice will show that you spent $1,000 on turkey breast for the month. But you mustn't stop there.

You should ask other questions:

- Should you have spent $1,000?
- What part of that $1,000 made it to guest checks?
- Were you paid for your portion of turkey breast?
- What amount was wasted?
- What amount was stolen or eaten by employees?

In an auto-parts store, employees don't eat the tires. But in a restaurant, employees might eat the turkey breast. Inventory theft includes employees eating in the restaurant or stealing food from the restaurant to take home. Some employees might purposely throw away beautifully sealed steaks, so they're unusable. Then they'll put the meat out with the garbage and come back at night, when they'll rifle through the dumpster to get their take. And they'll feed their family or sell it to somebody else.

As a restauranteur, you know your food cost from your invoices. Your accountant tells you, for example, you spent $1,000 on turkey breast. In the previous month, you only spent $500. Do you know what accounts for the difference? Unless you're controlling your inventory effectively, you won't know, and that's a problem not just limited to turkey breast. It also includes other kinds of meat, liquor, produce, and baked goods. It's every piece of inventory that goes into your business. The restaurant business is the only one in which the inventory spoils. A tire on the shelf at an auto-parts store doesn't spoil; a tire is not going to be eaten. It could be stolen, but typically auto-parts businesses keep tight controls on their inventory.

Theoretical Food Costing

In the world of restaurants, the only way to combat food cost is to generate your theoretical food cost. Every menu item in your restaurant should have, in theory, the ingredients that make up that item.

Let's say you offer a turkey club sandwich on your menu. Your turkey club sandwich should have six ounces of turkey breast. If you build a recipe in the system, every time a server rings up a turkey club, it will indicate six ounces of turkey breast will be used to create the sandwich. There's another recipe for a hot-open turkey sandwich that gets twelve ounces of turkey breast. You enter that into the system, so when someone rings up a hot turkey sandwich, it will indicate twelve ounces of turkey breast was used. You build your theoretical recipes not just for your sandwiches but also for your entrees and drinks.

You can, in theory, note everything that goes into making a drink, such as three ounces of Coca-Cola and three ounces of Chivas Regal. In practicality, most restaurants just record the important items. Three ounces of Coca-Cola wasted is minor compared to three ounces of Chivas Regal.

It's best to start each month with your current inventory. You'll begin by asking yourself: *How much turkey breast do I have on hand?* This requires counting your inventory. You must have either a manual or an automated system in which you go into your warehouse or cooler to determine how much turkey breast you have on hand. Let's say you start the month with ten pounds of turkey breast, and then you buy 100 pounds of turkey breast. The 100 pounds you bought will be on the invoice.

> **Of all the restaurants that use the POS system, only 20% use the inventory control piece. But the restaurants that use inventory control get results.**

At the end of the month, you count and determine you have five pounds of turkey breast left. You started with ten pounds, added 100, so that's 110 pounds, minus the five pounds remaining. That's easy math: 105 pounds of turkey are gone. In short, you're doing a very simple mathematical equation: The amount you start with plus the amount you bought minus the amount left over. The difference is your actual use.

If you have theoretical food costing in place, here's how it works: Because you've built a recipe for everything that includes turkey breast, your computer system will show all your sales for turkey breast that month, based on your theoretical recipes. So, in theory, you should have used ninety-eight pounds—seven pounds of which are not accounted for. Those seven pounds missing could be due to a recipe miscalculation, over portioning, theft, or spoilage. It's important to remember you'll never have 100%. In other words, there's a tolerance restauranteurs live with: an amount of unaccountable inventory that is acceptable. You must determine your own tolerance.

Perhaps your business is okay if you run at a 10% tolerance. Let's say as a restauranteur, you lost seven pounds of turkey breast. That's at the high end of your tolerance, but you'll see what happens next month. Next month, you're only missing five pounds, and the following month you're up to six again. You're still within the acceptable range. The next month you determine you lost twenty-five pounds of turkey. Is that a red flag? Of course, it is. You know on average you can run at five to seven percent loss to make a profit. So, when your loss jumps to twenty-five pounds, what will you do? You'll investigate and identify the problem. Your problem might not be limited to turkey; you could also have a problem with, say, sirloin steaks or Grey Goose vodka. That's part of the inventory process. When I look at the chains we do business with, the owners building successful restaurants have nailed this process.

Sadly, small entrepreneurs don't typically do this. Instead, they go with the old method of looking at what they spent and hoping they're within range. If they have an issue with their inventory, they're unable to pinpoint the problem.

Theoretical food costing is a discipline. It's a regimen that requires counting your inventory every week. And the person doing the counting must be held accountable to ensure accurate numbers. Let's say your manager takes ten pounds of turkey breast for his kid's barbeque. Then he fudges the numbers when he's doing inventory control. Nothing is worse than dishonest people who steal from you, but at least you have an indicator. You know everything's been at five or seven pounds, but now—under your new manager—it has jumped to seventeen pounds. With inventory management, you know you have a problem.

The inventory controls can also help you see what you're selling out on the floor, so you don't overbuy your product or prepare too much food. For example, if you make a big batch of guacamole and don't use it all, it goes to waste and costs you. Inventory controls help you track the waste and enable you to purchase the right quantity of avocados and other ingredients for the guacamole.

Larger chains can do inventory transfers to efficiently manage their inventory. Let's say you're a bigger chain and store number five has excess inventory, while store number seven needs ten pounds of turkey breast. Store number five then transfers turkey breast to store number seven. That way they minimize waste.

You don't have to be a large-chain restaurant to use inventory control. You should implement it from the outset. It's built into the system we work with; it's a tool that's available and very effective. There's resistance, because it takes work to effectively use inventory control—but it's worth the effort. What you put in is what you get out. Restaurants that use inventory control get results.

Let's revisit the turkey club sandwich example. The recipe would include two slices of wheat bread, two portions of tomato, and a slice of cheese. But you don't have to go into that level of detail. You could simply input your most expensive item—the turkey breast. So, you would have a recipe for the club sandwich, but turkey breast would be the only thing you'd track in the system.

If you have anything bottled, that's the simplest recipe. For a bottle of wine, the recipe is easy: one bottle of wine. To maintain inventory control over your bottles of wines is a no-brainer. But what happens, especially with restaurants that open and start making a profit, is they become intoxicated with their success and don't see the need for tight inventory control, even with simple items like bottles of wine. After the initial buzz dies down, and they face the challenges of becoming a real restaurant, they falter and sometimes fail.

If you were selling Rolex watches, would you count them? Of course you would—likely in the morning and at the end of the day. In the case of many restaurants, owners aren't valuing their products— the lettuce, tomato, bread, and the turkey breast. But they should, because inventory is money.

Inventory Control at the Bar

Because the highest mark ups are at the bar, inventory control should most definitely be used there. We often recommend if you're going to do anything, do it with the high-ticket food items and at the bar, because that's where you make most of your money. The problem with the bar is the bartender can easily give himself a shot of vodka or give one away. Then at the end of the month you wonder, *Why are my vodka costs up?*

Paul, who used to work for us, owned his own restaurant and became a sales consultant for us. His bar/restaurant wasn't doing the full inventory process. At some point, he noticed one month his Grey

Goose vodka costs had gone up by $300 or $400. He looked at the POS sales reports, which tracked his vodka sales. He realized that well vodka sales were extremely high and the Grey Goose not so much. He figured out one bartender was helping his friends by serving them Grey Goose and ringing up well vodka. It was as if he had decided to give his friends a Rolex watch, while charging them for a Casio or Timex, with the hope they'd give him a good tip.

This can easily happen at the bar, because the bartender and the customer have a direct relationship. In the kitchen, it's more complicated. A server orders food, which prints on a ticket so the chef can prepare the food. When the food is ready to be served, the chef gives the food to the server, who in turn delivers it to the customer. Bar transactions are simply between the bartender and the customer, so it's easier to give away drinks with no one noticing.

Many scams can occur at the bar. After you have implemented inventory control at the bar, you know how much liquor you started with. Let's use Grey Goose as an example. You know how much Grey Goose you started and ended with. You've been tracking it, and the inventory looks good, but you notice something strange: your inventory is okay, but your sales for Grey Goose are down. Why?

The bartender knows Grey Goose is a hot seller, so he's decided he's going to cut into your business. The bartender brings in his own bottle of Grey Goose to sell. He pours from his bottle, takes the cash, rings up no sale, and stuffs the money in his tip jar. The customer is happy because he got his Grey Goose. You are happy the bartender hasn't stolen your inventory. In fact, your inventory looks good. In other words, you still have your Rolex watches. But you didn't know your employee would be selling them off his arm in your establishment.

The bottles are part of the bar's décor, so who's going to notice there's one more bottle of Grey Goose? Obviously, you have a thief in your business, but he doesn't see himself that way. He might rationalize like this: "The owner is a successful guy who owns two houses, and I'm struggling, so he's not going to miss a few hundred dollars' worth of vodka sales I could make on this bottle."

You're controlling your inventory. You know how much Grey Goose you purchased and how much you ended up with. So, although your inventory system is going to catch most things, it's not going to catch this instance, where the bartender brings in his own bottle for sale. The customer doesn't care. When she gets her drink, she hands the bartender cash to pay for her drink. All the while, the customer doesn't know it's a scam.

> Successful restauranteurs are getting an economy of scale, they're negotiating their price so their chicken breast is less expensive than your chicken breast, and they're doing inventory control, ensuring they stay within acceptable margins to protect their profits.

Digital surveillance will help you determine exactly what's happening at the bar. When all else fails, look at the video; it tells you everything. We will cover this in more detail in the chapter on digital surveillance. When you have a video system tied into the POS, you will be able see your bartender grab and pour the Grey Goose, walk over to the touch screen, and touch no sale. You'd then confront the bartender and ask, "Why did you hit no sale whenever you served Grey Goose?"

Most POS systems will have reports on the number of no sales. A no sale is a function available for things like when a customer asks for change for the jukebox. You hit no sale, the drawer pops open, and you can make change. It opens the drawer without ringing anything up. It's a valid function, but one that has been abused. As a quick check at the end of a shift, you can look at the amount of no sales that a bartender did. If you run a cash-out report, and you see one bartender has three no sales each night, another has two no sales each night, and a third has twenty-seven no sales each night, it's obviously a huge red flag.

Purchase order control also applies when you are buying your turkey breast from a major purveyor. You negotiate a price with your representative and agree to pay five dollars for a pound of turkey breast. When your first invoice comes in, you make sure you are charged the correct price. Then you get busy running your restaurant and assume the price remains the same, so you don't check your invoice. But the price creeps up over time. One day you notice you're paying $8 per pound for turkey breast. You wonder, *How did that happen?*

With a purchase order control system, your last purchase price is entered. When you enter the purchase order, the purchase order gets sent out. When you get an invoice, the system will check it against the purchase order, and it will alert you when there has been a price change. It lets you know if you have a problem. You'll get your representative on the phone and say, "What is going on here? I thought we negotiated five dollars a pound for turkey breast."

> **It's wise to use a food costing system that compares your theoretical usage to your actual usage, rather than relying on your accounting system.**

A customer was using theoretical food costing with purchase order control and receiving, and they noticed the cost of chicken wings was going up. They wondered what they were doing wrong and went back to check everything. They discovered the purveyor, who used to include thirty-two pieces in a bag, had gone to twenty-eight pieces without telling them. At a busy restaurant, no one would detect the difference between twenty-eight and thirty-two chicken wings just by looking at the bag. When they looked at their food usage report—what they started with, what they had purchased, and what in theory they should have used—they found out they had been shorted by the purveyor. Bottom line: It's not only employees who can steal from you; vendors can too.

That is the other key to using the inventory. You may know you have a problem, but you don't know how to determine what it is. The inventory control piece pinpoints the exact problem, because the variance jumps off the page.

It's wise to use a food costing system that compares your theoretical usage to your actual usage, rather than relying on your accounting system. Even the mom-and-pop businesses have that. They're buying a certain amount of turkey breast, it's coming in on an invoice, and they're writing a check for it. That's their real food cost. Their theoretical food cost is what they should be using—based upon their recipes.

In my tenure of working with restaurants and POS systems, I've noticed most people see restaurants as a very simple business. They think it's such a cinch and that anyone can open a restaurant. For instance, a retired accountant decided he'd open a restaurant in Coral Springs, Florida. The restaurant was his baby. He wanted to be the front guy at the restaurant, shaking hands and kissing infants. But he got hosed big time, because he didn't consider key factors like inventory control. His restaurant lasted only three or four months. It happens so often, because the restaurant industry looks easy from the outside. Investors assume all they need to do is open the doors, people will come, and they'll make a ton of money. It's a lot harder than that, but they would have a much better chance by protecting their investments with a POS system and putting inventory control practices in place.

There are so many factors that contribute to a restaurant's success besides food quality, service, and ambiance. Successful restauranteurs know their stuff. They've only survived because they're doing *most* of this. When—in fact—the large, successful chains do *all* of this.

Remember, lack of inventory control is one of the major reasons restaurants go out of business. It occurs when you don't keep track of your inventory and, as a result, you spend too much on your inventory—then fail to get the return required to keep you in business. When you've invested time, energy, money, and passion into your restaurant venture, inventory control with a POS system is an excellent way to safeguard your investment.

Preventing "Buddy Punching" and Other Strategies for Managing Labor

Using the POS system's tools will enable you to manage labor effectively to maximize your return on investment.

Labor management is like inventory management in that how you manage labor can make or break your restaurant. Whether you're a restaurant owner or an investor, using the POS system's tools will enable you to manage labor effectively to maximize your return on investment.

In the restaurant business, the fixed costs include rent and the executive's salary; the variable costs are food and labor. If you're not careful, your labor cost can spiral out of control. Typically, restaurateurs look in their rearview mirror instead of planning ahead. At the end of the month, your accountant looks at your numbers and says, "Do you know you spent $13,000 on labor costs?" You're shocked because you usually spend $10,000. If you're not tracking your labor costs, you'll have no idea why you spent $3,000 more that month and simply vow to do better the next month. Does this sound familiar? If you have labor control using the POS system, you can pinpoint exactly where the problem is.

Preparation is key. If you're a general going into battle, you must plan for the number of troops and necessary resources you'll need to get the job done. If you're running a restaurant, you should identify in your business plan how much you want to spend on labor. Even with the best plan, you must control labor, because there are ways to fudge time. For example, employees can manipulate controls by working just seven hours—but making it look like they worked eight. A manager, trying to be gracious, may dole out extra hours to staff, thinking the owner will never know. The manager can overschedule so there are too many employees on the floor, meaning more employees are being paid for doing less work. And, inevitably, some employees will angle for overtime. In that case, you're spending times one and a half when you could be spending times one for the same labor. These are some of the areas that become problematic when you're not effectively controlling labor. That's what labor management is all about.

To manage labor, you must first ask yourself, *What's my plan?* The next question should be, *How do I stick to my plan?* If your restaurant is open thirty days each month, you have thirty days in which you could potentially blow up your plan. Therefore, you should check throughout the month to ensure you're on target. To do this, you must first have a system in place. You typically start with a labor schedule. You'll map out a schedule that identifies the people you need to run your restaurant including cooks, helpers, busboys, servers, bartenders, and managers. With the proper tools, you can lay out a schedule that will show you all the players in every department. In that plan, you will detail their hourly labor costs. You know how many hours each day they will work. In theory, if you staff everyone, you will know before the month starts what the labor costs for that month will be.

You also know on average how much you earn in sales. If you're running a start-up restaurant it's more challenging, since you must accumulate this information over time. But if you're running a restaurant that has been in business for a while, you will have a feel for how much business you're going to do in a week.

Let's say, on average, you do $20,000 each week in sales. In fact, if you're a good restauranteur, you know how much you bring in daily. Typically, Mondays and Tuesdays don't bring in much. You make the bulk of your money on Thursday, Friday, and Saturday. Most likely, you need the most employees when you're making the most money. Your plan includes the number and types of employees you need and when you need them.

You'll calculate your labor cost up front by asking, *What is my target labor cost against my sales?* It's simple math. You can see your labor cost as a percentage of sales. For example, based upon your projected sales, you anticipate a 30% labor cost. You know from your business plan if labor is at 30% of sales, you'll make money. If you go up to 40%, you'll break even or lose money. Therefore, as a business owner, you must maintain labor at 30%.

You need a trusted tool to help you stay on track. Good POS systems tie everything together. When working with a system that incorporates labor management, you would use the scheduling feature, having entered all employees by departments, including your cooks, sous chefs, servers, managers, busboys, and hostesses. On Friday and Saturday, you will need more servers, so you adjust the schedule, and the system will compute your labor hours and your costs against your sales. This feature also lets employees know their work schedules.

> **A time clock that enforces the schedule will keep people honest.**

Next, you'll enforce the schedule. How does this work? A good system will have a timekeeping feature that interfaces with the schedule and the POS. The system knows the schedule. When an employee clocks into the system, the time clock will review the schedule and determine Johnny, the sous chef, is supposed to be on the clock at 9:00 a.m. Instead, he's coming in at 8:30 a.m. Without a timeclock that enforces the schedule, he can punch in at 8:30 a.m., pour himself a cup of coffee, pick up the sports page, and hang out until his shift starts. Guess who's paying for that? You are.

A time clock that enforces the schedule keeps people honest. It will also give Johnny a grace period and notify him he's punching in thirty minutes early. When he punches in, Johnny will see a message: "Your start time is at 9:00 a.m. The system will start calculating your time from 9:00 a.m."

With the time clock enforcing the schedule, is your job done? Not yet.

You built a beautiful, streamlined schedule, but then life happens. Becky needs a schedule change because her great aunt is visiting from out of town. So, you assign Tony to her shift. Then Frank has a family emergency and needs someone to cover for him, so he asks Tony.

It's Thursday and Tony is scheduled for the rest of the week. That means by Friday he's already into overtime. Tony doesn't mind, as he's saving up for a new truck. A good system will warn you there's a potential overtime problem. We call it the Overtime Prediction Report. With a good system, you will look at the remaining schedule for the week and see Tony is going to be over forty hours. So, you'll tell Tony you need to reschedule him. Al will take some of his shifts, because he is not an overtime risk.

Preventing Buddy Punching

That said, there are ways to scam even the best systems. One common example is the buddy punch—the act of one employee clocking in another employee who hasn't begun his or her shift.

On a POS system, there are three ways to get into the system. The most common is with a user number that's typically the last three or four numbers of the user's Social Security number. Let's say you have an employee named Jack with the number 917. Jack comes into work and punches his number into the time clock. It checks his schedule, and he's on the clock. Jack's girlfriend, Ashley, also works at the restaurant. One day, Ashley is running late and asks Jack to punch her in with 644. Jack does a buddy punch and enters her number. Now you're paying Ashley, who's not even at work yet.

> **Fingerprinting is now available in the POS system with fingerprint readers that interface with the POS. Without it, you could be buddy punched to death.**

Fingerprinting is now available in the POS system with fingerprint readers that interface with the POS. This eliminates buddy punches. Without it, you could be buddy punched to death.

With a timekeeping time-clock system, you'll have the ability to edit the time clock. Managers must have the option to go in and make exceptions. For example, a server named Lena has been at work since 9:00 a.m. It's 11:30 a.m., and Lena says she forgot to punch in. The manager will ask her what time she got in and does a time clock adjustment in the system. Or perhaps Lena came in at 9:00 a.m. but didn't punch in until 11:00 a.m. Again, the manager would adjust her time clock. Just like the scenario in management controls, where a manager removed a poorly-prepared steak from a check, making exceptions is a normal function that can get out of control if not watched. Management exception reports within labor would show you this manager is making frequent adjustments for Lena. In the restaurant business, friendships and romances often drive managers to make exceptions.

For the system to work, you must look at the reports. A good time-keeping system will put reports into a file that allow you to print the exceptions. Let's say you're the owner who is looking at the Exception Report; you see this manager is making an inordinate amount of exceptions for Lena. You can use this report as the basis for questioning your manager and finding the underlying cause. Or perhaps you have an employee who's perpetually late, and you decide to let that person go. Exception reports in a good labor management system give you a dependable audit trail.

> Exception reports in a good labor management system give you a dependable audit trail.

The scheduling feature also monitors employees punching out. For example, Trevor, an employee who was scheduled to work until 4:00 p.m., tries to punch out at 6:00 p.m., but is unable to because the system shows he was only scheduled until 4:00 p.m. Trevor must ask a manager to make an exception that enables him to punch out at the later time. The manager will know if Trevor was working or just hanging out with his buddies at the end of his shift. The manager controls the scheduling feature instead of permitting employees to punch in and out whenever they please.

With salaried positions, you could have managers punch in and out to see if they're worth their salaries. However, owners don't usually ask managers to punch in and out, because restaurant managers often work more than forty hours per week.

Occasionally, managers will claim the controls are bad for morale. Generally the person who makes that assertion is the person who's stealing from you. In one instance, a client had a manager who was badmouthing the system. It turned out he was making exceptions for his girlfriend. As accountability increases, some employees won't like it. But the ones who don't like it are often the ones running scams. Honest people will usually comply with your wishes.

Poorly managed inventory and labor are two of several reasons restaurants don't maximize their profits or sometimes go out of business. These are variable costs you can control. If you control them to your advantage, it will increase your profit. But if you let them get out of control, they will eat into your profit—possibly putting you out of business.

For example, let's say you're a five-million-dollar-a-year restaurant, and you're spending one million dollars on food costs. That's just under $90,000 each month in food costs. If you can shave off three percent, or roughly $2,700 per month, those are real dollars you can add to the bottom line.

Your car has a speedometer to tell you how fast you're going. Similarly, you need controls in your restaurant to help you identify what you're doing right and wrong. A POS system helps you identify why your labor cost is up. With these controls, you can see that for a given month you spent $13,000, but you should only have spent $10,000. You can see you spent too much on overtime pay. You know there's a problem, what the problem is, and how to address it.

Another key to effective labor management is having access to historical information. It's challenging for a startup, because they don't have historical data yet. But for a restaurant that has been in business for a while, they have a history of their sales, inventory, and labor.

Let's look at the ways historical data can benefit your restaurant. Two of the busiest days in the restaurant business are Valentine's Day and Mother's Day. With historical data, your restaurant can go back to previous Mother's Days and look at the amount in sales and cost for labor. As Mother's Day approaches, wouldn't it be nice to be able to go into the system and see your labor usage, as well as your top sellers? A good system can help you plan, target, and prepare for the coming Mother's Day by looking at historical trends.

In anticipation of Mother's Day, you look at your past sales numbers to plan for staffing. You decide to put three extra people on the floor—a sous chef, a cook, and another floor manager, because your sales will warrant that. You're not staffing from your gut, which may or may not be correct. You're making staffing decisions from a numbers standpoint; you're going to do $10,000 more in business. With historical information, you can make better business decisions. Your decisions are based on numbers and analytics, rather than your intuition.

> **Your gut may serve you well when your restaurant is the new trendy place and the economy is strong, but when times are lean and tough, such as after 9/11 or during the bubble in 2008, how you manage labor can mean the difference between profitability and operating in the red.**

Using the scheduling feature, you can enter the numbers and assess the analytics. For example, you think you need three extra employees on Mother's Day. When you look at it from a budgeting standpoint, you notice the extra employee will raise you to an unacceptable number in the labor percentage. You decide you can make do without the other person and reduce it to two.

If you have a POS system in place to manage your variable costs, it will get you through the down times. And even if you're doing well, it will help increase your profit margin.

When a restaurant owner is earning decent money, he may not see the need for a POS system with inventory and labor controls. For example, let's say Eddie the Manager is sending the remote owner $15,000 a month—which keeps him happy. The owner thinks, *I'm* *doing great; I'm earning $15,000 a month from my restaurant. I don't have to do much, because Eddie is running it for me.* Little does he know he could be getting a check for $30,000 a month. Eddie knows the owner's tolerance and has figured out how to get more for himself. This system helps remote owners by protecting their profit margins.

As with inventory control, labor control requires a regimen of inputting data and assessing analytics. The POS system has built-in alerts, but in many cases, you must review the numbers to stay on top of labor management. It's like any good habit, such as brushing your teeth. When you wake up in the morning, you don't think, *Oh, it's just too much work to brush my teeth; I'm skipping it.* You know if you don't brush your teeth, your teeth will fall out, or you'll get gum disease. You develop a routine of brushing your teeth to get the desired health results. Similarly, you must stick to a daily, weekly, and monthly labor control regimen to get the desired business results.

In the last chapter, you learned to build your recipes one at a time and then count the inventory on a weekly basis. With labor, you must input schedules and generate reports to ensure you maintain the desired percentage of labor costs.

Know what you can control and what you can't. For instance, you may have little control over insurance costs for your full-time employees. In general, to minimize labor costs, you must find the right balance of full versus part-time employees. Full-time employees will be more committed to your restaurant and usually will not need to be replaced as often as part-time employees. But these cost savings will be offset by the cost of the benefits full-time employees are entitled to.

Finding experienced, qualified employees is the key to success for any restaurant. But even the most qualified people will need some training. It is important to provide proper training for the whole staff, starting with the hosts and including the cooks and servers. With a good crew in place, regular staff meetings are critical to identifying issues you need to resolve to keep everyone operating efficiently.

How you manage labor can make or break your restaurant. Whether you're a restaurant owner or an investor, using the POS system's tools and developing regimens to monitor the analytics will enable you to manage labor effectively—to maximize your return on investment.

Eye in the Sky: Video Surveillance

With digital surveillance- the POS system keeps an eye on your business 24/7—so you don't have to.

We've all seen segments on the nightly news in which a video shows a hold up at a convenience store. Upon seeing the gun, the clerk panics, empties the cash drawer, and the perpetrator flees with the money. With the crime captured on film, it is much easier to get a criminal profile and ultimately catch the perpetrator.

We had a customer in the Florida Panhandle who caught a sexual predator, because he had a camera system in place. The guy followed a woman out of the restaurant and attacked her in the parking lot. The police searched the archived video from the digital video recorder (DVR). The suspect was identified inside the bar from the video, and he was also seen leaving the bar with the victim. The police were able to arrest the suspect with the evidence captured on the DVR.

From a general liability standpoint, it makes sense to have a video surveillance system to keep track of the normal mishaps, as well as crimes that may occur in the restaurant business—slips and falls, sexual harassment, robberies, and thefts. When dealing with the public and restaurant employees, it's smart to have some type of camera system or digital surveillance in strategic locations, such as at the cash drawers, the front and back doors, and the parking lot.

So, if a customer says he slipped in your parking lot, you can refer to the video to determine if it is a real or false claim. Or perhaps a server accused the manager of sexual harassment on her Tuesday night shift. You can view footage from that night and see she's gathering her things and walking out the door with no harassment incident. It's a no brainer to have digital surveillance—technology that safeguards your company from frivolous lawsuits and keeps your profits in your pocket.

Surveillance technology is everywhere. For example, you can have a system installed outside your home that allows you to remotely monitor your front door. When someone rings the doorbell, and you're away from home, you'll get a notification and the ability to talk to the person at your front door.

With surveillance in your restaurant, you want to be able to see the transactions taking place at the terminals. You could have it installed at the clock-in terminal and, most importantly, at the bar terminals. If you have cameras pointing at the bar, the register or touchscreen, the system can record the transactions happening at the POS and overlay that information on the video. This links the specific transaction to the video.

> We had a customer in the Florida Panhandle who caught a sexual predator because he had a camera system in place. The guy followed a woman out of the restaurant and attacked her in the parking lot. The entire scene was caught on camera and used by the police to capture and convict the rapist.

Here's how it works: When you're looking at the video of the bartender using the touchscreen, what he's touching is displayed on the video in a digitized format. If he touches Budweiser, the screen records Budweiser. In other words, whatever he touches is inserted into the video. You see him ringing up items in the video, and you see—side by side—the specific drinks he's ringing up.

From a remote location, you can connect to the internet and watch your bartenders in action. We've heard stories in which the owners catch their bartenders putting on a show. They'll jump up on the bar and perform a song and dance for customers. They'll do crazy stuff, which is against your policy. You can keep an eye on what's going on remotely through the cameras. When you tag it to the POS, you can see exactly what your bartenders are ringing up.

Let's revisit the case of the bartender who brings in his own bottle of Grey Goose to sell. As an owner, you maintain tight control on your inventory, but this scam can't be discovered with inventory control alone. Every time a customer orders Grey Goose, the bartender is going to pour from his bottle, take the cash, hit no sale, and put the money in his tip jar. With the video alone, you can see the bartender pouring Grey Goose, but you don't know if it's his bottle or yours.

> **You can keep an eye on what's going on remotely through the cameras. When you tag it to the POS, you can see exactly what your bartenders are ringing up.**

The customer gives him cash and tells him to keep the change. The bartender then walks to the POS and touches no sale, which you can't see, because his back is to the camera. But on the video linked to the POS system, it flashes no sale. He didn't account for the Grey Goose; it's not part of your sales. Even though you can't see what he's touching, you can see what's on the touchscreen, because it's inserted in the video. Therefore, you know exactly what he's doing.

The problem is not every owner watches the cameras. Typically, you are not going to sit and watch the bartender's every move, but a good POS system will record the number of no sales for each bartender. The videos have a playback feature that allows you to go back and view some or all the footage. Typically, the videos will store for thirty days. In the event of an incident, you can go back to see what happened. It's timestamped and recorded.

Bartenders run a scam with deletes that can be caught with video surveillance. There are two kinds of deletes: one before you send the order and one after you send an order. For example, you go into Burger King. When you order a Whopper, the employee at the counter punches Whopper into the system. But then you change your mind and order a Double Cheese Burger. The employee hits the delete button to cancel the Whopper. The employee's ability to delete an item before sending an order is a normal transaction in restaurants and bars, because customers change their minds about their orders.

This is also a common occurrence in bars. You order a Bud Light, but then change your mind and order a Coors Light instead. The bartender will delete the Bud Light and ring up the Coors Light before the order has been processed. In other words, the bartender hasn't closed the transaction. It's best to streamline this process at the bar, because you don't want to slow the bartender down with a cumbersome delete process. But when it comes to high-ticket items in a restaurant, like a lobster dinner, you must have a more involved process in place. If the server touches "lobster dinner" on the touchscreen and sends that order to the kitchen, but then the customer changes her mind—or the dinner was unsatisfactory—you'll have a more involved process to remove the item from the check. Once something has been sent, a manager is usually required to delete the item. There's typically an audit trail for this type of delete. This is considered a "delete after". But at a bar, because it's instantaneous, we let bartenders delete items.

One scam bartenders run works like this: A bartender will ring up two four-dollar beers for the customer. The POS terminal shows the two beers, which adds up to eight dollars—as displayed on the terminal. He hands her the two beers and says to her, "That's eight bucks." She hands him a ten-dollar bill and says, "Keep the change." He takes the customer's money and then hits delete twice, which takes the beers off the screen—like it never happened. He then puts the cash in his tip jar. You've lost the sale and depleted your inventory.

Most systems will track the delete after the transaction has been processed. Only a few will track the "delete before". Here's why you want to track the delete before. Typically, your bartenders average three to five deletes per night. Let's say you have a new bartender named Tony who people love. You look at your report and see he's got thirty deletes a night. You clearly need to look into the problem. If you have a digital surveillance camera, you can go back to the shift Tony worked and look at what's happening with every no sale. In the video, you see him put two Budweisers on the bar. He turns around and touches delete twice on the touchscreen, so the transaction never happened. The money goes into the tip jar. Or perhaps he hits no sale and puts the cash in the drawer, which he counts out at the end of his shift. Any surplus will go in his pocket.

One way to track this is to look at the alerts and at the digital surveillance when they're tied together. Normally, you'll access the digital surveillance if something suggests you should, like if Tony the Bartender has thirty deletes. You probably won't have a manager review the entire video every day. Instead, you're looking for exceptions. You're looking for alerts, and when you receive them, you will want to go back and

> **When you spot check your restaurant with digital surveillance, you'll keep your employees on their toes.**

drill down to see what's happening. If you're an owner, you're not going to sit and watch the video all night, but you could spot check. For example, you could see when you spot check that an employee isn't wearing his uniform correctly. You'd call the manager with the feedback, and the employees would realize you have an eye on them. They never know when you're watching, which keeps them on their toes.

Another thing that happens in the restaurant business, especially for remote owners or if you have a weak late-night closing manager, is the manager closes everything down but stays and parties. He thinks, *My shift is over, but why go home when there's a fully stocked bar and a pool table here? Now I can take it easy and have a few drinks.* If you're not doing inventory control and the night shift team hangs out at the bar and helps themselves to your inventory, you can catch it on video.

One of the management controls we recommend with bartenders is called the "blind cash out".

A blind cash out is when someone other than the bartender counts the drawer. It's one of the checks and balances in a restaurant. You see it all the time at the grocery store. Someone comes and pulls a cashier's drawer. You don't see it as much in bars, but it's the same principle: you don't want the person responsible for the drawer counting the money.

You shouldn't let bartenders pull their own cash outs. A cash out shows what they rang up for the day—their total numbers and what they should have in the drawer. Because they can enter a no sale to open the drawer, if you allow them to view the report ahead of time, they can pull money from the drawer. In a blind cash out you don't let them see their numbers. If bartenders are playing games, they might end up with excess cash in the cash drawer. If you let them count the drawer themselves, where do you think the money goes?

Maybe you have a new bartender who forgot to ring something up or rang it up incorrectly. Whatever the reason, the money in the drawer is the house's money. If the report indicates there should be $100 in the drawer, but there's $120, the surplus goes to the house. Obviously, if the drawer is short, you'll have a conversation with the bartender. It's standard practice for the manager to demand the bartender hand over the missing twenty dollars.

When you have a situation with too much money in the cash drawer, it could be a red flag the bartender is playing games or perhaps not ringing up every item sold. When you look into the problem, you can use digital surveillance and reporting to identify a trend. Usually, you can nail a dishonest bartender by catching him in the act.

A digital surveillance system may show bartenders doing short pours, which is common among bartenders, especially with inebriated clients who are less likely to notice. When bartenders do short pours, they can use the excess liquor in another drink, charge the customer, and pocket the cash. You're likely to see short pours with video surveillance, but it's a bit more difficult to track than other scams.

Some restaurants allow bartenders to comp a certain amount per night. The owners don't care who the bartenders give those drinks to, but they must make sure to ring them up so when inventory is taken, so the liquor is accounted for. Owners give bartenders some reign to give drinks away, but they must account for it. The comp is punched into the system on a comp check. It's good business to comp loyal customers on their birthdays or holidays. But if you offer too many drinks on the house, keep in mind—the house may not survive.

> **If you offer too many drinks on the house, keep in mind—the house may not survive.**

The POS interface gives you the ability to overlay what's happening at the POS onto the video, so even if you normally wouldn't be able to see what's happening in the video, the items being rung up can be seen. The bartender has his back to you, and he's doing something you can't see, but whatever he's touching shows up on the video.

The POS digital surveillance interface gives you the technology you need to monitor your restaurant remotely and ensure your profits are going into your pocket and not someone else's. It enables you to minimize liability for false claims and gives you peace of mind. With digital surveillance, the POS system keeps an eye on your business 24/7—so you don't have to.

SWIPING AND DIPPING: CREDIT CARD PROCESSING

CREDIT CARD CHIP TECHNOLOGY IS BEING IMPLEMENTED IN THE U.S. TO OUTPACE CRIMINALS AND HACK ERS. IT'S A NIP-AND-TUCK RACE WITH NO CLEAR WINNER IN SIGHT.

Credit card processing in the United States is a little crazy right now because to make a payment, you sometimes swipe and in other cases you dip. Dipping—the credit card industry's term—means inserting the end with the chip into a slot, chip side up. You leave it there until the transaction is complete. Many merchants do not have software to support chip card technology, so you don't know which you're supposed to do: swipe or dip.

In the early to mid-2000s, as people and businesses were flocking to the internet, hacking and stealing credit card information was on the rise. The number one way to steal credit card information was to write down someone's card number and later use the stolen credit card number to perform a transaction. With the advent of eCommerce, consumers were able to input credit card information on vendor websites and purchase things. Hacking into these sites provided another way for thieves to steal credit card numbers.

Another way to steal credit card information is with a mobile scanner called a "skimmer." A restaurant server takes a customer's credit card to pay the check, scans the card with the skimmer, and returns the card to the customer. The mobile scanner stores the customer's credit card information. The server repeats this process with countless cards and later downloads all the scanned credit cards to the criminal who's paying the server.

On a larger scale, tier one merchants, including Target, Home Depot, and other national chains, were targeted by criminals. Tier twos are regional chains, tier threes are thriving local businesses, and tier fours are mom-and-pop shops. When these big chains were breached, tens of millions of people in the United States contacted the credit card companies in a panic about fraudulent charges.

The way internet credit card hacking works is like this: Once hackers penetrate a business' system, their hacking malware sniffs the network looking for number patterns. The program is written to recognize and grab credit card numbers, along with the expiration dates and all other pertinent information, then store it secretly in a hidden file. Once enough numbers and associated data are compiled, the program is designed to wake up and send the information out through the internet to the digital criminal masterminds, who then sell the credit card numbers on the black market. Soon after, your credit card company would call and ask if you bought, say, a motorcycle in Hungary. And, unless you had become a Hog Warrior in Budapest, you would say, "No," which would trigger the credit card company's fraud protection measures. The credit card company would see these fraudulent transactions coming in, and they would review their records to see what store or entity was the common source of these card numbers. They'll figure out which business had these credit card numbers processed at their business. They'll determine the common source or place of business where the breach occurred.

Credit card companies weren't prepared for the widespread fraud and criminal activity. Before credit card theft became a huge problem, when a Visa customer would see that charge from Hungary and think, *Hey, that's not my charge*, the credit card company would resolve the issue only by removing the charge from the customer's bill. This satisfied the consumer. Then the company would compensate for the losses by charging everyone higher interest rates or fees.

What happens now is credit card companies must issue you a new card when your card has been breached. The expense to the credit card companies of absorbing fraudulent charges and issuing new cards has been immense, adding to their cost of doing business.

> **Credit card companies came up with payment card industry (PCI) standards requiring merchants to protect their businesses from breaches, thereby shifting the liability to the merchant. The credit card companies required merchants to be PCI compliant and to have a firewall.**

In response to the ballooning costs of doing business in the early 2000s, Visa, MasterCard, American Express, Discover, and JCB got together and came up with Payment Card Industry (PCI) standards that require merchants to protect their businesses from breaches, thereby shifting the liability to the merchant. The credit card companies require merchants to be PCI compliant by following a set of guidelines. Here are the current guidelines of this program:

PCI Data Security Standard – High Level Overview	
Build and Maintain a Secure Network and Systems	1. Install and maintain a firewall configuration to protect cardholder data. 2. Do not use vendor-supplied defaults for system passwords and other security parameters.
Protect Cardholder Data	3. Protect stored cardholder data. 4. Encrypt transmission of cardholder data across open, public networks.
Maintain a Vulnerability Management Program	5. Protect all systems against malware and regularly update anti-virus software or programs. 6. Develop and maintain secure systems and applications.
Implement Strong Access Control Measures	7. Restrict access to cardholder data by business need to know. 8. Identify and authenticate access to system components. 9. Restrict physical access to cardholder data.
Regularly Monitor and Test Networks	10. Track and monitor all access to network resources and cardholder data. 11. Regularly test security systems and processes.
Maintain an Information Security Policy	12. Maintain a policy that addresses information security for all personnel.

Once the PCI standards were in place, if the merchant were breached and not fully PCI-compliant, they could be charged for forensic audits, hard drive replacement and confiscation, legal fees, and/or fines. The contract a merchant signs with a processor says the merchant is agreeing to maintain PCI compliance.

What are the small guys without lawyers supposed to do? Many owners sign without reading the fine print. The terms of the contract state if you get breached, you're responsible. The credit card companies audit your system. They conduct a forensic analysis on your system, and if they determine you do not have the necessary security, you are held responsible. Restaurants have gone out of business because of the fines imposed. Not only that, when a restaurant is breached, it hits the newspaper and customers swear off the restaurant. They think, *I'm not going there again, because they screw up cards. Even if it doesn't cost me, it would be a hassle to get a new card.*

> **When you sign a contract with a credit card company, you must read the fine print, because you're claiming you have a system in place that prevents you from being breached. If you are breached, it is your responsibility. First, you will be fined by MasterCard and Visa. Then they will audit you and ask for your hard drives.**

While the implementation of the PCI-compliance program helped fight credit card fraud, criminals have also stepped up their game. As a result, credit card companies have become even tougher by adopting credit card embedded chip technology known as Europay, MasterCard, Visa (EMV). EMV is a global standard for cards equipped with computer chips and the technology used to authenticate chip-card transactions.

While migrating to this new technology protects consumers and reduces the costs of fraud, implementing the chip technology has been a huge hassle and cost for restauranteurs. Implementation depends on your POS—where it connects to the platform, the platform itself, the processor, and the bank. You must have a special reader, which will vary according to systems and companies. The readers and payment process are expensive and slower. No doubt hackers are busy trying to figure out how to hack systems with chip technology.

Another thing that has happened in our industry is something called "friendly fraud." If a merchant doesn't have the software and hardware to process a chip embedded card, they can still swipe a customer's chip card. Systems that do not have EMV chip readers can still swipe the card via the magnetic strip. We've been told that the magnetic strip will not be on credit cards within five years.

> Some of our customers lose five or ten thousand dollars a month in charge backs, because the banks refuse to dispute. The bank's position is: If you don't have a chip reader, that's not our problem. It's yours.

Here's how the friendly fraud game works. If your business swipes an EMV chip card (rather than inserting the chip) and the client disputes the charge, the business will receive a charge back from their bank. The credit card processor sets the rules. The banks resolve it by refunding the customer and then charging the merchant. It doesn't even matter if you have a signed receipt. Some of our restaurant owners lose five or ten thousand dollars each month in chargebacks, because the banks refuse to dispute the charges. The bank's position is: If you don't have a chip reader, that's not our problem. It's yours.

Another way to protect yourself is by making sure you're doing business with a Qualified Integrator and Reseller (QIR certified). Being QIR certified means the organization has the knowledge and skills to securely install Payment Application Data Security Standard (PA-DSS), validated payment applications into merchant environments that comply with the PCI Data Security Standard. Vendors that should obtain QIR certification are those that configure and/ or install POS software, payment applications, and terminals for merchants.

A QIR-certified vendor like Pinnacle helps restaurants become compliant. Some restaurants, such as the tier-four mom-and-pop shops, opt to roll the dice. If they are breached, they'll be fined, and that could put them out of business. If you're dealing with a QIR-certified vendor who sells POS systems, you can opt in or out of the services they provide, but if you opt out you must provide those services yourself. In other words, there's no getting around the fact that you must be compliant.

> **If you're dealing with a QIR-certified vendor who sells POS systems, you can opt in or out of the services they provide, but if you opt out, you must provide those services yourself. In other words, there's no getting around the fact that you must be compliant.**

Today, almost all businesses accept credit cards, so it is your responsibility to protect your systems from being hacked or breached. On top of PCI compliance, you must have chip readers and the proper software to avoid the friendly-fraud chargebacks. Some industries, like gas stations, have been given a temporary exemption, but not restaurants.

Another credit card scam leverages rewards programs. One of our customers had an employee who was collecting cash checks and closing them out to her credit card to receive the rewards credit. The employee was likely thinking, *No foul here. I'll take the $100 cash. I can use the cash, and I'll just swipe my card to pay.*

If it's a big rewards card, 4% could get charged against the transaction. It costs the merchant to process credit cards. If the merchant does $100 in business, they don't get $100 back from credit cards. The credit card companies take their fees out of the transaction. The greater the rewards, the higher the fees, so the merchant actually pays for some of those reward points. When the server takes the $100 cash and puts it in her pocket, the restaurant may only get ninety-six dollars back from the credit card company.

The restaurant industry is moving toward a system where the credit card doesn't leave the patron's sight. The pay-at-the-table method, mobile wallets, and mobile payments are the emerging technology solutions. Increasingly big chains, like BJ's Brewhouse, are using mobile payment. When your check is ready, the mobile app sends an alert for you to open, and you add your tip and pay without ever giving anyone your card. It's quick, seamless, and secure.

Tipping has always been the most difficult transaction for full-service restaurants. When a customer purchases something at Walgreens, they stick their chip card into the reader and complete the transaction. But with restaurants, the customer opens a tab with a credit card, then the employee adds items to it. When the customer is ready to go, the server closes the tab and then goes back to add a tip, after which the bartender must again open and close the tab. It's not a simple one-step transaction.

The pay-at-the-table method and mobile wallets are cloud based. You're connecting from the POS to the Cloud. Products like PayMyTab and EMV readers are much more secure, because the readers encrypt all the information. It decodes only when it reaches its destination. The token, created at the POS, goes out to these apps.

The token can't be hacked; if hackers penetrate it, the information is unreadable. The token that passes between the two applications is encrypted. Also, when you insert your card with a chip, it's encoded and being relayed as encrypted data. In contrast, when you use the swiping method, the reader sends the actual card numbers down the network, so the data is vulnerable.

> **The restaurant industry is moving toward a system where the credit card doesn't leave the patron's sight. The pay-at-the-table method, mobile wallets, and mobile payment are emerging technology solutions.**

If you have a mobile wallet, you can complete the transaction using your phone. If you don't want to pay that way, servers can run your credit card tableside, allowing you to see your card the whole time. When the pay-at-the-table unit displays the check, you just dip your card to complete the transaction. When the transaction has been completed, the server hands your card right back to you.

As a restaurant owner, you must make sure you have credit card security systems and processes in place to protect your bottom line. Without these measures, you are vulnerable to credit card hacking schemes and, if breached, answerable to credit card companies. Unless you have the recommended security apparatuses, you are liable for any breaches, and this could cost you your business.

SMART DINING: THIRD PARTY INTERFACES

IF ANY RESTAURANT WITH A SIGNIFICANT TAK EOUT

BUSINESS CALCULATES A RETURN ON INVESTMENT-

THEY WILL FIND ONLINE ORDERING IS THE WAY TO GO.

In the digital age, customers want the ability to place an order with a restaurant while on the go—ideally from their phones or tablets. But it means restaurants must offer a mobile ordering system to meet customer demands. Doing so typically increases order volume and profits and decreases errors and waste.

Apps and programs that supplement your POS system, like online ordering, interface with the POS and enhance the restaurant business. They enable customers to order by phone from their homes or other locations. If your POS is interfaced, all transactions are traceable, trackable, and flow through one system.

Interfaced Ordering System

If your ordering system is interfaced with POS, the order flows through the app and the system prints the order in the kitchen. Even though it's two systems, it acts like one, because it's interfaced.

On the other hand, if you have an online ordering system that's not interfaced, it creates inefficiencies. For example, when a customer places an order, the system generates a fax that is sent to your restaurant. Restaurant employees must then take the fax and enter it into the POS.

Online ordering reduces the need to have an employee at your restaurant taking orders. The mature POS systems offer these interfaces. Some of our larger customers find their own third-party apps and then interface with the POS. With an online ordering system, you can increase your food sales by doing more takeout. Chinese restaurants are famous for takeout, but most haven't caught onto online ordering. They stop the action in the restaurant when they're taking orders over the phone. In contrast, many chain restaurants, like BJ's Brewhouse, have implemented online ordering. They've discovered the cost of having someone answer the phone, and entering the order into a terminal is outweighed by the advantages of online ordering.

These systems will cost you, but much less than paying an employee to monitor the phone. In fact, the return on investment is incredible. It's important to choose a good system to interface through the POS, so you don't have to balance two systems. Credit cards come through the POS when customers pay online with their credit cards. Online orders are included in total receipts, so your online sales and online credit cards are in the same place as your restaurant sales. If you have separate systems, it will inevitably result in more errors, more mistakes, and more labor.

If any restaurant with a significant takeout business calculates a return on investment, they will find online ordering is the way to go. Ten years ago, it was very expensive. The prices have come down to the point independent restaurants with the right POS and online ordering system can compete with the big chains.

From home, a customer places an order from their phone, and it goes directly through the restaurant's POS—just as if they're ordering in the restaurant. Although designated as an outside order, it goes right through. Some of the systems even include an algorithm for pickup time. For example, a customer places an order at 7:30 p.m. Based on the order volume, the pickup time functionality reports the customer's order will be ready at 8:20 p.m.

Another emerging trend is third-party food delivery. Before this trend, a big expense for restaurants that deliver was staffing delivery drivers. There was the potential for delivery drivers to get into accidents or to steal money when they were handling cash. This is where companies like UberEATS and Grubhub come in. The customer orders on their phone and then the Uber-EATS or Grubhub delivery person picks it up from the restaurant and delivers it to the customer. The delivery company charges restaurants for the service. Some of the delivery services are integrated. So, for example, employees in offices who don't want to go out for lunch will be able to order through an app instead.

> ### Food Delivery Interfaces
>
> **Interfacing with companies like UberEATS and Grubhub can transform your delivery function by increasing sales, decreasing marketing costs, and freeing up capital to enable you to hire new employees to meet the demands.**

When your menu is featured on the third-party apps, it will generate new business and enable loyal customers to enjoy your food more often. Linking with delivery companies gives you the capacity to deliver food to your customers quickly, while maintaining the best possible food quality. You can also track orders on the floor, right to a customer's door.

Another type of popular third-party integration is with reservation and waiting systems. These systems offer online reservations, reservation management—both via phone and online—and table optimization. In the late 1990s and early 2000s, many companies offered online reservations as a way for restaurants to increase their business. It was a crowded space, but at the end of the day, only one survived. The legacy reservation system charges quite a bit for its service, so some restaurants love it, while others don't. Competitors are popping up that offer similar table reservations and waiting systems. Call aheads and in-restaurant waiting are connected to the POS. Some reservation systems are not only expensive, but when you link your restaurant website to them, they field your customers to their website and give your customers access to all the restaurants in the area. This can drive customers away from your restaurant— right into the hands of competitors.

Other reservation systems are entering the market. If you're an established restaurant with a loyal clientele, customers making a reservation are not thinking, *Wow, I just found a great place on this reservation system. Let's have dinner there.* They're planning to go to your restaurant anyway, so you're paying the reservation system to give you business you already have. If you can eliminate the pricey reservation system, you can slash $600-800 each month from your expenses and install a reservation system that's integrated with a website you control. That's another best practice. New apps will connect to your POS, giving you the ability to manage your own reservations without a huge fee. For a much lower fee, your customers can access your reservations without viewing any other restaurants in the area. There's no charge per reservation. You just pay a base monthly fee—about $100 or $150 a month—and then you can make a thousand reservations with no upcharges.

Some of the apps have a waiting system functionality. When a customer comes into your restaurant and discovers there's a wait, the waiting system allows her to add her name to the waitlist, and she can then use her phone to track her place in line and see when she will be seated.

When you give your guests waiting for a table the ability to monitor their place in line, you'll increase sales at the bar. Customers will think, *We're number four in line to get seated, so we have time to get a drink.* This is much more pleasant than hovering around the hostess stand and asking the hostess when they'll be seated. Customers can monitor the waitlist themselves. When it's their turn to be seated, they are notified on their phone. That's the next big wave.

> **When you give your guests waiting for a table the ability to monitor their place in line, you'll increase sales at the bar.**

As with Uber ride sharing, customers can do everything from their phones. Some waiting system apps include a loyalty plan. If you install beacons in the store, you can pick up the customers with the app on their smartphones who are part of your loyalty plan. The beacons will know when loyalty customers have arrived in the store and will know where they're seated. The manager can then locate the loyalty customers to ask about their meal, give them some extras, and thank them for coming. It also can accumulate points that can be turned into rewards points. Many customers want to use their loyalty points for VIP treatment that enables them to get to the front of the line—or secure the best table in the house to watch the Super Bowl.

It is impossible for any POS manufacturer to develop all the apps and systems required for running a restaurant, including online reservations and online ordering. Therefore, they have an open API that enables other programs to interact with the system. An open API is a publicly-accessible application programming interface that provides developers with programmatic access to a proprietary software application or web service. It creates an open system. This is how most POS manufacturers integrate with all third-party apps. As with credit cards, we deal with all credit card processors. They flow in and out of the engine of the POS system. As a restaurant owner, you can pick up or turn on or off whichever apps you want to use for your restaurant.

As innovations in third-party apps and programs emerge, and you selectively incorporate them into your restaurant's business model, you will increase control over all inputs and outputs, all while improving food quality, growing your customer base, offering service and delivery innovations, and boosting profits.

Takeaways

Chapter 1

- When looking at POS functionality, look to minimize errors and omissions and to eliminate theft and scams. These are the two primary profit killers.

- When it comes to pricing control, it's best to have a system that handles all your pricing options that vary by day and time of day.

- The POS records all the details of the transaction, the specific guest check, the server, and the manager who performed the function. These functions increase restaurant revenue.

- A superior POS system will make it impossible for servers to order the wrong thing, due to multiple layers of options and modifiers set for each of your menu items.

- The vendor or VAR should provide regular updates to the software, continually fixing any bugs and delivering improvements. There should be help with training and emergency support if the system fails.

Chapter 2

- It's important that the system not only report the voids, but also show who performed them, the date and time, the server, and the check number.

- If you're evaluating systems for your restaurant, you should ensure audit trails is one of the features included, not just to show you overall deletes, but also who performed the delete, for what server it was performed, and the reason for the deletion.

- To be effective, there should always be an audit trail on a discount or coupon.

- A good system will generate any sales reports owners and managers want to see, such as overall sales and sales of food, alcoholic beverages, and nonalcoholic beverages.

- The management controls in the POS system enable you to track, monitor, and analyze sales, including performance monitoring of your menus and sales staff.

- A good software system organizes the information your accountant will need to make tax return preparation much less painful.

Chapter 3

- Lack of food cost control is one of the major reasons restaurants go out of business. It occurs when you don't keep track of your inventory.

- In the world of restaurants, the only way to combat food costs is to generate your theoretical food costs.

- Because the highest mark ups are at the bar, inventory control should most definitely be used in the bar.

- When you've invested time, energy, money, and passion into your restaurant venture, inventory control with a POS system is an excellent way to safeguard your investment.

Chapter 4

- Using the POS system's tools will enable you to manage labor effectively to maximize your return on investment.

- Fingerprinting is now available in the POS system with fingerprint readers that interface with the POS. This eliminates buddy punches.

- Poorly managed inventory and labor are the top two reasons restaurants go out of business.

- Finding experienced, qualified employees is the key to success for any restaurant. It is important to provide proper training to the whole staff, starting with the hosts and including the cooks and servers.

Chapter 5

- When dealing with the public and restaurant employees, it's smart to have some type of camera system or digital surveillance in strategic locations, such as at the cash drawers, the front and back doors, and the parking lot.

- It's a no brainer to have digital surveillance—technology that safeguards your company from frivolous lawsuits and keeps your profits in your pockets.

- Bartenders run a scam with deletes that can be caught with video surveillance.

- With digital surveillance, the POS system keeps an eye on your business 24/7—so you don't have to.

Chapter 6

- One way to steal credit card information is with a mobile scanner called a skimmer that stores the customer's credit card information and later downloads all the scanned credit cards to the criminal.

- In response to the ballooning costs of doing business in the early 2000s, Visa, MasterCard, American Express, Discover, and JCB came up with Payment Card Industry (PCI) standards that require merchants to protect their businesses from breaches, thereby shifting the liability to the merchant.

- Protect yourself by making sure you're doing business with a Qualified Integrator and Reseller (QIR certified).

- Watch out for credit card scams that leverage rewards programs.

- Today, almost all businesses accept credit cards, so it is your responsibility to protect your systems from being hacked or breached.

Chapter 7

- Online ordering reduces the need to have an employee at your restaurant taking orders. These systems will cost you, but it will be much less than paying an employee to monitor the phone.

- It's important to choose a good system to interface through the POS, so you don't have to balance two systems.

- When your menu is featured on third-party apps, it will generate new business and enable loyal customers to enjoy your food more often.

- An emerging trend is third-party food delivery. Linking with delivery companies gives you the capacity to deliver food to your customers quickly, while maintaining the best possible food quality.

- Another type of popular third-party integration is with reservation and waiting systems that offer online reservations, reservation management—both via phone and online—and table optimization.

- If you can eliminate a pricey third-party reservation system, you can manage your own reservations without a huge fee, and your customers can access your reservations without viewing any other restaurants in the area.

- The next big wave is apps with a waiting-system functionality. When you give your guests waiting for a table the ability to monitor their place in line, you'll increase sales at the bar.

- An open API is a publicly-accessible application program-ming interface that provides developers with programmatic access to a proprietary software application or web service. It creates an open system.

- Selectively incorporate third-party apps into your restaurant's business model to increase control over all inputs and out-puts, all while improving food quality, growing your customer base, offering service and delivery innovations, and boosting profits.

Glossary of Terms / Acronyms

API

Application Programming Interface (API). An open API is a publicly accessible application programming interface that provides developers with programmatic access to a proprietary software application or web service. It creates an open system that can integrate with third-party apps.

Audit Trail

A paper or electronic record of the step-by-step history of transactions. For example, an audit trail tracks voids, deletes, and comps. It tracks the specific employee who performed the void, delete, or comp, as well as the manager and the server associated with the check.

Buddy Punching

A time-clock system used to track employee work hours can be abused by employees who punch in their fellow employees, such as a friend who is running late. Fingerprinting with fingerprint readers that interface with the POS system eliminates buddy punches.

Chargebacks

A friendly fraud can cost a business thousands of dollars, if the business has not yet converted to chip readers for credit cards. If a customer swipes an EMV chip card and later disputes the charge, the banks will refund the customer and charge the business back without recourse, since it didn't have a chip reader.

DVR

Digital video recorder (DVR) is the video storage component of a digital video surveillance system. A video surveillance system allows management to track mishaps and crimes that may occur in the restaurant business. Digital surveillance technology safeguards your company from frivolous lawsuits and helps detect employee scams.

eCommerce

Electronic Commerce (eCommerce) is the buying and selling of goods and services over an electronic network, usually the internet. Since consumers can input credit card information on vendor websites to purchase things, hacking into them provides another way for thieves to steal credit card numbers.

Food Delivery Interface

Food delivery interface integrates restaurants with third-party food delivery companies like UberEATS and Grubhub. The customer orders on their phone (or with an app) and the UberEATS or Grubhub delivery person picks it up from the restaurant, delivers it to the customer, and charges restaurants for the service.

Interfaced Ordering System

An interfaced ordering system is integrated with the POS, so that orders from an app or over the phone flow through the system and print the orders in the kitchen.

PCI Standards

Payment Card Industry (PCI) standards require merchants to protect their businesses from breaches, thereby shifting the liability to the merchant. Credit card companies require merchants to be PCI compliant by following a set of guidelines.

Point of Sale (POS)

Computer-based systems that range from basic systems that can perform the simple operation of printing a price on a check to more complex systems that offer sophisticated controls and processes to increase the bottom-line profitability for your restaurant.

POSitouch

The flagship POS product of Restaurant Data Concepts that is featured in this book. POSitouch is branded as the most robust POS system in the food service industry.

Qualified Integrator and Reseller Certified (QIR certified)

A certified organization has the knowledge and skills to securely install Payment Application Data Security Standard (PA-DSS)—validated payment applications into merchant environments that comply with the PCI Data Security Standard.

Theoretical Food Costing

Theoretical food costing is the process of using a computer system to keep track of every ingredient that goes into all the food and drink items for a restaurant. This provides management with tight inventory controls. Among other things, these inventory controls can help you see what you're selling out on the floor, so you don't overbuy your product or prepare too much food.

Value-Added Reseller (VAR)

A VAR or POS dealer represents the software developer and provides clients (restaurants) with all the software and hardware along with training installation and on-going support.

84812280R00052

Made in the USA
Columbia, SC
26 December 2017